SURVIVING DIVORCE

A LAWYER'S COMMON SENSE GUIDE

TO WHAT YOU SHOULD KNOW

BEFORE, DURING, AND

AFTER A DIVORCE

JOHN HOLLINS, JR.

EVEREADY PRESS
1817 Broadway Nashville, TN 37203

Surviving Divorce
A Lawyer's Common Sense Guide
To What You Should Know
Before, During, And After A Divorce

Copyright © 2011 by John Hollins, Jr.

Cover & book design by Jadyn M. Stevens / Eveready Press

Printed in the USA
ISBN: 978-0-9826118-4-5

Legal Disclaimer

I am licensed to practice law only in the State of Tennessee. All legal references in this book are based on Tennessee law. The law in your state or jurisdiction may be vastly different. If you have a legal question, please contact a reputable attorney, whom you trust, in the jurisdiction where you live.

More important, this book is not intended to be a substitute for hiring an attorney. Nothing in this book should ever be construed as rendering legal advice in any way whatsoever. Never try to use this information as a do-it-yourself divorce manual. This book is a common sense guide to help assist any person affected by a divorce to better understand the process from start to finish. As stated above, if you have a legal question, please contact a reputable attorney, whom you trust, who practices law in your jurisdiction. Never attempt to use this information instead of hiring a lawyer.

- John Hollins, Jr.

EVEREADY PRESS
1817 Broadway Nashville, TN 37203

DEDICATION

❧

This book is dedicated to my father, **John Hollins, Sr.**, a true Southern gentleman in every sense of the word. He has been a family law attorney for over five decades and has mentored me for over two decades. During that time, I have learned the importance of integrity, honesty, and judgment. Dad led by example. Most importantly, he taught me how to practice law – the right way.

This book is also dedicated to my dear wife, **Laura**, who has provided unconditional love, understanding, and support to me and our twin daughters, **Emily** and **Meredith**, when we needed it the most. Her unselfish devotion to our family has helped make us all better people. Thank you for sitting with me at our dining room table and helping me "cut and paste" our way through the first draft of this book. Your steadfast encouragement was what I needed to stay focused and composed. You are a treasure to me, our daughters and to everyone who knows you.

ACKNOWLEDGEMENTS

This book would not have been possible without the help of my dear friend **H. Jackson Brown**, who wrote the blockbuster *Life's Little Instruction Book* series. He inspired me to write a common sense book that would help anyone who is affected by a divorce. He graciously donated his time, wisdom, and encouragement to see this project through completion. This book would have never been possible without his superb writing skills. For that I will be eternally grateful.

Thank you **Martha DuBose** for sharing your mastery of the English language and providing your brilliant editing skills. You have the unique ability to edit a manuscript and literally make the words come alive. You are simply the best!

Special recognition goes to **Jadyn** and **Mike Stevens**, owners of Eveready Printing & Press in Nashville, TN. They are experienced, knowledgeable, and accommodating. Their printing quality is second to none. Thanks guys!

Many thanks to my legal assistant **Julie Potts**, who has typed and edited over two dozen drafts. Your devotion has helped me see this project through to completion.

For over two decades I have been blessed with the good fortune of practicing law with and against many top-notch attorneys and judges. In addition to my father, other attorneys have helped mentor me along the way. Thank you to **James G. Martin, Jr.**, Judge of the 21st Judicial District of Tennessee; **Edward Yarbrough**, former United States Attorney for the Middle District of Tennessee; **Robert L. Jackson, Edward P. Silva**; and **John Wagster**. You never compromised your professionalism no matter what adversity you faced. Thank you so much for your helping hand.

I am also indebted to everyone who helped me edit the final draft of this book. They include family, friends, and attorneys. Thank you to **Marlene Eskind Moses**, Esq., Past President of the American Academy of Matrimonial Lawyers, **Dana Gentry**, **Ben Raybin**, and **John Hollins, Sr.**

A special bow to **Roxie Gibson**, author of the successful *Hey, God!* series of books. You are one of the few Saints on earth. You have provided moral, spiritual, and educational guidance from the time you taught me in kindergarten at Oak Hill School in Nashville, Tennessee, four decades ago. Thank you for your encouragement along the way in completing this project. If everyone could model their life after you, we would all be in a better place. I am blessed for having known you all these years.

I want to thank all of my current and former law partners and associates for all their support, guidance, and friendship over many years. Thank you to **David Raybin**, **David Weissman**, **Vince Wyatt**, **Sarah Richter Perky**, **Ben Raybin**, **Jackie Dixon**, **Pat McNally**, **Jim Weatherly**, **John Norris**, and **Russ Heldman**, former Judge of the 21st Judicial District of Tennessee.

A special salute goes to my crackerjack legal assistant **Robyn Gornicki-Davis**. She keeps me organized, on schedule, and grounded. Your attitude is great, and your outgoing manner keeps us all on the straight and narrow. You rock!

I would be remiss if I didn't acknowledge the rest of my current legal assistants, **Brenda Davis**, **Ashley Farrell**, and our accountant **Jason Lankford**. I am fortunate to work with such a highly competent staff. You make my job easier and more enjoyable!

Prologue

Regrettably, far too many marriages end in divorce. Every divorce case is unique because each person involved in a divorce is unique. No one is ever prepared for all the issues that are part and parcel of divorce. I know. I have been a family law attorney for more than two decades and represented hundreds of people going through the process. *Surviving Divorce* is the product of what I have learned and the wisdom I have gained.

I decided to write this book after a conversation with my friend H. Jackson Brown, the author of many bestselling collections of wit and wisdom. Jackson told me how he was inspired to write his first blockbuster, *Life's Little Instruction Book*, as a gift for his son, who was leaving home for his freshman year in college. As I listened to Jackson, it dawned on me that maybe I could help my clients by writing down what I know. I began on Christmas Day in 2008, sitting at the kitchen table with a yellow legal pad and a pen. Dozens of legal pads and multiple rough drafts later, *Surviving Divorce* was complete.

As might be expected from a practicing attorney, this book includes practical information about the legal process and its complications. It is also intended as a common sense guide to dealing with the physical, emotional, and spiritual stresses that divorce puts on individuals and their families. My goal is to provide a straightforward and easy-to-use manual to assist those affected by divorce to get through the inevitable trials and tribulations with their hearts, minds, and dignity intact.

Drawn from my own knowledge and experience, *Surviving Divorce* is my gift to everyone – divorcing spouses, their children, their families, and their friends – touched by this difficult choice. Hopefully, it will make the process easier and the future brighter.

TABLE OF CONTENTS

THE BEGINNING

THE CALM BEFORE THE STORM

INTRODUCTION

1. The decision to divorce is one of
    the most significant decisions you
    will ever make.

    ❧

2. Divorce does not mean you are a
    failure as a spouse, a parent, or a
    person.

    ❧

3. Divorce is a traumatic experience
    for everyone involved. Nothing
    about it is pleasant or easy.

    ❧

4. Divorce can be emotionally and
    economically devastating to you,
    your   spouse, your children, and
    your entire family.

5. Divorce and child custody cases involve many complex issues because they involve couples who were (or still are) madly in love with each other. Oftentimes they grow to hate each other just as passionately.[1]

&

6. There is a thin line between love and hate.

REALITIES

7. It is easy to get married. It is hard to stay married.

&

8. Children are a permanent commitment. Marriage may not be.

9. Life is not fair. Divorce is not fair. The legal system is not always fair.

⟳

10. We live in an imperfect world. Bad things do happen to good people, which means that sometimes good people get bad results in divorce cases.

⟳

11. Perfect marriages don't exist. Perfect spouses don't exist. Perfect parents don't exist. Perfect children don't exist. Dysfunction exists in every household. It's just a matter of degree.

⟳

12. Most spouses' expectations about how great life will be after a divorce are unrealistic. The grass is not always greener on the other side.

GETTING ADVICE

13. Don't allow your family and/or friends to create unrealistic expectations about your case. Every case is different.

❧

14. Be extremely cautious about following the legal advice of "well-meaning" family members and/or friends who are recently divorced.

❧

15. In most cases, the advice you get from your friends and family is worth exactly what you paid for it. Absolutely nothing!

16. Consider seeking the advice of family members and/or friends that you would trust to raise your children.

❧

17. Avoid relying on older and grown children for advice, since this is often a way that spouses manipulate children into taking sides.

❧

18. Legitimate divorce support groups sponsored by a mainstream church and/or qualified health care professional are usually helpful.

Process

19. The laws of physics also apply in divorce cases – for every action there is an equal and opposite reaction. You cannot control the divorce process. If you are a controlling person, the divorce process will frustrate and disappoint you. Parties who simply want to punish their spouse and delay the case will waste a lot of time and money and accomplish nothing.

∽

20. Stay focused on the legal issues, not the emotional ones. Uncontrolled bitterness and hatred can easily lead to long, expensive, and unnecessary court battles.

21. In most cases you will not get everything you want. Your spouse will not get everything he or she wants either.

22. Fighting over matters of "principle" can be costly and frustrating. So can fighting over minutia. Pick your battles carefully. For example, don't spend five hundred dollars in attorney fees over a fifty-dollar problem.

23. Spend less time worrying about who is right and more time worrying about what is right. So do the right thing. Always take the "high" road. You will never regret it.

24. Never cry wolf. True emergency situations are rare. Very few issues need immediate attention.

Responsibilities

25. In most cases you are not as innocent as you claim, and your spouse is not as guilty as you claim. There is always another side to your story.

❧

26. We all have shortcomings. It is human nature to try and hide them. We tend to look at things the way we want to see them and not the way they really are.

❧

27. Accept responsibility for your conduct, good or bad. Admit your mistakes. Be honest with yourself. Be honest with your lawyer.

CIVILITIES

28. Getting through a divorce with your dignity and personal reputation intact should be your ultimate goal. Using the divorce process simply to punish a spouse is likely to boomerang and hurt the punisher.

29. Don't mistake an act of kindness from your spouse as a sign of weakness.

30. The way you handle yourself during the divorce will affect your relationship with your spouse and children forever.

31. A true test of a person's character is how he or she deals with a dispute over money. Money and things will not make you happy. You must make yourself happy.

YOURSELF

32. No one has to suffer alone. Don't be afraid or embarrassed to ask for help.

❧

33. Stay in touch with your friends and family. Try to limit the discussion about your case.

❧

34. It is natural to grieve the loss of your relationship with your spouse and/or children.

35. If you pray, pray often. If you go to church, go often.

❧

36. If you need spiritual counseling, talk to your pastor, priest, rabbi, and/or advisor often. Consider enrolling yourself and your children in counseling. Seeking a counselor is a sign of strength, not weakness.

❧

37. There is no shortcut to healing.

❧

38. In most cases, extreme emotions are only temporary. It is normal to experience extreme emotions such as anger, fear, guilt, loneliness, frustration, helplessness, sorrow, resentment, regret, and depression. If you experience extended, severe mood swings, you should consult with a counselor or a doctor.

39. Excessive use of alcohol and/or drugs (legal or otherwise) will only make matters worse. Seek professional help if your life is out of control.

⤜

40. Don't believe everything you hear.

⤜

41. Don't be too "thin skinned."

⤜

42. Don't feel sorry for yourself.

⤜

43. Don't take yourself too seriously.

⤜

44. Self-righteousness will not serve you well.

45. Don't tolerate unacceptable behavior. Stand your ground!

～

46. Never jeopardize your integrity for anybody or anything.

～

47. Never falsely accuse your spouse of misconduct, especially adultery.

～

48. Don't say it if you don't mean it.

～

49. Resist the temptation to waste your time on things you cannot control.

～

50. Create a calm, loving, peaceful atmosphere in your home, especially if your spouse still lives there.

Your Spouse

51. Never underestimate your spouse. Never underestimate your spouse's lawyer.

52. Spouses tend to focus on the bad times and forget about the good times.

53. Remember that the time you spend hating your spouse deprives you of those moments of happiness you shared together. All couples have shared good times.

54. Don't forget that there was a time when you were passionately in love with your spouse.

55. Don't forget that you picked your spouse to be your mate for life.

❧

56. Don't forget that you chose your spouse to be the parent of your children.

❧

57. If the other parent is a bad person whom you have grown to hate, remember that he or she will always be your children's father or mother.

❧

58. Never tell your spouse you wish you had never met or married him or her.

❧

59. Never tell your spouse that he or she is nothing but a loser.

60. Never tell your spouse that you hate him or her.

⁓

61. Never tell your spouse that you wish he or she were dead.

⁓

62. Always treat your spouse, their friends, and their family with courtesy and respect.

⁓

63. Respect your spouse's role as a parent.

⁓

64. Never interfere with your spouse's ability to obtain the children's school records, including report cards, attendance records, names of teachers, class schedules, and standardized test scores.

65. Never interfere with your spouse's ability to participate in your children's extracurricular, sports, or school events.

✒

66. Try to accommodate your spouse's request(s) to modify a visitation schedule if the request is reasonable.

✒

67. Give your spouse at least 48 hours notice of all of your children's extracurricular activities, school activities, and athletic activities.

✒

68. Give your spouse notice of all children's doctors', dentists', and other health care appointments.

69. Never threaten to move out of state with the children to intimidate your spouse or to gain leverage in your case.

∾

70. Never undermine your spouse's, your spouse's family's, or your children's religious beliefs.

∾

71. Never have any communication with your spouse or about your spouse that may be perceived as threatening or abusive. This includes phone calls, voice messages, e-mails, text messages, and postings on any social network such as Facebook, Twitter, and MySpace.

CHILDREN

72. Divorce can be more difficult on the children than the parents. What is best for your children should always come first. What is best for you is not always best for them. It may take your children months or even years to adjust to the divorce.

⁓

73. Children naturally want to love both parents. In most cases, children don't understand why their parents divorced.

⁓

74. Most children hope that their parents will get back together.

75. It is usually best to break the news about divorce to the children in a meeting where both parents are present. Your children will often blame themselves. Assure them they are not responsible.

❧

76. Your children will eventually ask you why you are getting a divorce. Tell them that you and your spouse are the ones responsible for the divorce. Your children will want to know if they will have a safe place to live, access to both parents, will go to the same school, and have the same friends. They want clear and honest answers.

❧

77. Tell your children that both parents love them very much and this will never change, but you and your spouse just can't live together.

78. Both you and your children will be embarrassed about the divorce. Don't be surprised if both you and your children experience a wide range of emotions, including anger, sadness, and resentment. It is important to take care of yourself and your children's mental and physical well-being. Early counseling may be beneficial, especially when both parents are involved.[2]

❧

79. If parents make every effort to effectively co-parent, it is less likely that the children will act badly. If you truly love your children, you will allow them to love the other parent. Remember, if you have children, you will likely deal with your spouse forever.

80. Spending quality time with your children when they are young should encourage them to want to spend more time with you when you are older. Parenting time spent with your children is never wasted. Children value your time much more than they value your money.

❧

81. Encourage your children to talk to you and listen carefully to their concerns.

❧

82. Encourage your children to have regular contact with your spouse. Encourage your children to visit the other parent even if you disagree.

❧

83. Don't listen to conversations between your children and the other parent.

84. Never discuss the details of the case when you can be overheard by the children.

~&~

85. Never discuss the details of your case with your children under the "excuse" that they need to know the truth.

~&~

86. Don't tell your children you're going to do something if you're not. Never make promises to your children you cannot or will not keep.

~&~

87. Never make derogatory comments about your spouse to the children, and never allow third parties to make derogatory comments about your spouse to the children.

88. Don't interfere with your spouse's court ordered time with the children. Spouses who do this may go to jail.

❧

89. Don't interfere with or try to cut short your children's telephone calls, e-mails, text messages, or other contact with your spouse.

❧

90. Don't confiscate your children's cell phone or terminate the cell phone service to prevent contact with your spouse.

❧

91. Never confiscate, destroy, or otherwise interfere with mail your spouse sends to your children.

92. Don't promise gifts to your children to encourage them to cut short your spouse's time and/or contact with them.

❧

93. Never bring your boyfriend/girlfriend around your children or take them to your child's sporting events, school functions, or extracurricular activities prior to your divorce.

❧

94. Never tell your children that your spouse is trying to put you in jail for violating a court order (even if they are).

❧

95. Never tell or encourage your children to lie about anything, and never tell them to keep a secret from your spouse. It may affect custody issues.

96. Never tell your children anything you do not want repeated. It might be used against you.

❧

97. Never tell your children that your spouse is not paying child support and/or alimony. It places the child in the middle of the dispute.

❧

98. Never tell your children they cannot participate in any activity because your spouse refuses to pay for it (even if it is true).

❧

99. Never argue with your spouse in front of the children.

❧

100. Never curse at your spouse in front of your children.

101. Never try to encourage your children to dislike your spouse.

❧

102. Never tell your children that your spouse would not have left if he or she really loved them.

❧

103. Never tell your children they don't have to visit your spouse if they don't want to.

❧

104. Never question your children about your spouse's activities.

❧

105. Never use your children to relay messages to the other spouse or to "spy" on your spouse.

106. Never alienate your children from your spouse and/or his or her family.

❧

107. Never ask your children where they want to live or whom they want to live with. It puts your children in a position where they have to choose between their parents.

❧

108. Visitation schedules should be made between the parents.

❧

109. Be flexible when formulating a visitation schedule.

❧

110. Resist canceling or modifying your parenting time with your children.

111. Leave your children out of all adult decisions related to the divorce.

❧

112. During the divorce process, don't let your guilt allow you to lower your expectations of your children or give them things you would not normally give them.

❧

113. Don't allow your children to play one parent against the other.

❧

114. Be aware that children experiencing divorce may be more likely to experiment with alcohol, drugs, and sex. Children may feel vulnerable and join the wrong crowd.

115. Parents need to closely monitor their children's grades and behavior. The best measure of behavior is how they act when you are not around.

❧

116. If you are not faithful to your spouse, your children may not be faithful to theirs.

❧

117. Don't be surprised if your children experiment with alcohol and/or drugs if you do.

❧

118. Parents who allow teenagers to spend time with their friends will enjoy a much better relationship.

SELECTING THE RIGHT LAWYER

119. Your selection of a lawyer is as important as your decision to divorce. A true professional will care about you as a person and not just as a client.

❧

120. Trust is the most important component in any attorney-client relationship.

❧

121. Remember, the same lawyer cannot ethically represent both spouses. It is always better if your spouse has a competent and experienced lawyer. If you can't afford a good lawyer, perhaps you should borrow the money.

122. Hiring a lawyer is like anything else –
you get what you pay for. If you're
diagnosed with a serious illness, you
don't hire the cheapest doctor you can
find. You hire the best doctor you
find. The same is true of lawyers.

123. Lawyers earn a good reputation by
blending talent, intelligence,
competence, judgment, and integrity.
A well founded reputation for
integrity is the lawyer's most
important attribute.[3]

124. Obtain the names of three reputable
lawyers from people you trust.

125. Investigate your lawyer's credentials
before you hire him or her. Begin by
reading the content of the lawyer's
website before the first meeting.

126. A lawyer should have an "AV" rating from the Martindale-Hubbell publication (www.martindale.com). Find out if he or she is a member of the American Academy of Matrimonial Lawyers (www.aaml.org) and if he or she is listed in the Best Lawyers in America publication (www.bestlawyers.com). Also find out if your lawyer is a member of the American College of Family Trial Lawyers (www.actl.com), and find out if he or she has a record of public discipline from your state Board of Professional Responsibility.

127. Meet with a lawyer before you hire him or her and ask how many cases he or she has tried in your judicial district. Your first meeting with a lawyer should be similar to attending a church service. If you do not feel more knowledgeable after you leave, he or she is not the right attorney. And remember, there's no such thing as a dumb question.

128. Ask the lawyer if he or she has ever been through a divorce and if he or she has a good relationship with many of his or her clients after the divorce.

❧

129. Ask the lawyer about the scope of his or her representation and whether it covers all the pretrial hearing(s), mediation(s), final hearing(s), appeal(s), and/or post-divorce hearing(s), and who will work on your case, including other lawyers and/or legal assistants.

❧

130. Don't hire a lawyer who "talks down" or patronizes you. Never hire a lawyer who guarantees results in court or who claims to have never lost a case.

131. Ask your lawyer about his or her fee structure. Most charge by the hour for the time they work on the case and charge in increments of one-tenth an hour to one-quarter an hour for all phone calls, e-mails, text messages, letters, and meetings. Longer phone calls, e-mails, text messages, letters, and meetings may be billed at one-half an hour or more.

❧

132. Be sure you clearly understand his or her hourly rate and the hourly rate of every other attorney and/or legal assistant who may work on the case.

❧

133. Ask your lawyer about his or her normal business hours. Most lawyers charge additional fees for working after-hours and on weekends.

134. Most lawyers require the payment of an initial retainer fee. A retainer fee is payment in advance for legal work to be performed at a later date. The retainer fee is typically deposited in a trust or escrow account from which they pay themselves for work performed. Ask if the retainer fee is refundable. Non-refundable retainer fees help insure that a lawyer will get paid for his or her time.

135. Ask your lawyer if there will be additional costs other than attorney fees for services such as court filings, court reporters, copies, faxes, long distance phone calls, computerized legal research, expert witnesses, and mediators.

136. Ask your lawyer if an expert witness such as a forensic accountant who values businesses; a real estate appraiser who values houses, buildings, or land; a personal property appraiser who values cars, boats, and furnishings, or a mental health professional who evaluates custody issues will need to be hired. Know the cost of the expert before he or she is hired.

137. Consult with your lawyer before hiring a financial advisor known as a "divorce consultant." Divorce consultants tend to be expensive and may hurt your lawyer's efforts to settle your case.

138. Ask your lawyer if he or she will pay for the expenses up front and bill you later or if you will be required to pay the expenses as they are charged.

139. Many lawyers require additional funds to be placed in a separate trust or escrow account to be used to pay costs and expenses other than attorney fees.

140. Ask your lawyer for an estimate of the total amount of fees and expenses to complete the case. Remember that the lawyer's estimate is made at the beginning of the case and could change dramatically depending on the difficulty and length of the case.

141. Most lawyers require clients to sign a fee agreement contract when the lawyer accepts a case.

142. Read fee agreements carefully. Be sure you fully understand them.

143. Always sign a fee agreement with your lawyer and retain a copy for yourself.

144. Lawyer fee agreements should contain the following essential elements:

a) Scope of representation
b) Hourly rate of each lawyer and legal assistant
c) Who will work on the case
d) Retainer fees – refundable or not
e) Funds advanced for costs
f) Lawyers' office hours
g) Resolution of fee disputes

145. Ask to receive monthly statements documenting the work on your case and a balance of your funds in any trust or escrow account.

WORKING EFFECTIVELY
WITH YOUR LAWYER

146. Divorce lawyers understand that people are not their best under the pressures of divorce. Your lawyer is there to keep your case on track, guide you through the process, and make the experience as painless as possible.

❧

147. Your lawyer should tell you the truth about your case and let you know when your expectations are unrealistic. Listen to your lawyer and pay attention to his or her advice, even when it's not what you want to hear.

❧

148. Your lawyer can't work miracles. He or she can only operate with the facts you provide, so always tell your lawyer the whole story – the truth and nothing but the truth.

149. In a divorce case, nobody likes surprises. To avoid being blindsided at any point, give your lawyer all the details from the very beginning. Hiding information can cause serious problems down the road.

～❧

150. Be courteous to your lawyer's receptionist(s), paralegal(s), legal assistant(s), and other employees. Your lawyer's staff is working for your benefit. If you have a complaint, confide it to your lawyer.

～❧

151. Remember that you aren't your lawyer's only client. Lawyers must spend a considerable part of every day in meetings, on the telephone, and responding to e-mails and text messages. Respect his or her time.

152. Make sure you have a legitimate reason to call your lawyer. Don't call just to "chit chat." He or she will bill you.

&

153. Make a list of questions before you call your lawyer. Also, keep your e-mails and text messages brief and to the point.

&

154. Most lawyers and/or their legal assistant(s) will bill you for every meeting, phone call, e-mail, and text message. Be wise.

&

155. Promptly return your attorney's phone calls and respond to his or her letters, e-mails, and text messages.

156. Always leave a callback number if your lawyer is not available.

❧

157. Good lawyers return phone calls. If your lawyer repeatedly fails to return your calls, find out why. Call his or her legal assistant and schedule a telephone conference or a meeting.

❧

158. If any problem develops with your attorney, discuss it with him or her immediately.

❧

159. Don't discuss your case with your lawyer in a social setting.

160. Unless you have a real emergency, don't call your lawyer after hours or on weekends. Your spouse being thirty minutes late getting the children home after a scheduled visitation is not an emergency. An example of a genuine emergency would be domestic violence by your spouse.

❧

161. Spouses often dislike their spouse's lawyer. Don't let this impair your judgment.

❧

162. Never make a false report about your spouse's lawyer to the state disciplinary board because you are angry. A false report could backfire and make it difficult to resolve your case.

163. A legitimate ethical violation by a lawyer should be reported to the state disciplinary board. Consult with your lawyer before taking any action.

❦

164. Never insist that your lawyer take an unreasonable position solely to punish or embarrass your spouse.

❦

165. Never speak badly about your lawyer or your spouse's lawyer. The mud you throw is as, if not more, likely to stick to you as to the lawyer.[4]

❦

166. If you disagree with your lawyer's advice, you might consider getting a second opinion from another lawyer.

167. Never consult with another lawyer about your case without telling your lawyer first. If you decide to consult with another lawyer, get your lawyer's written permission first.

❧

168. Pay your attorney bills on time. Nothing will kill your lawyer's enthusiasm for your case faster than an unpaid bill. Lawyers have a hard time thinking about your case when they are not getting paid.

❧

169. In case of financial difficulty, talk with your lawyer about a payment plan. Prompt payment is a great motivator. Remember that your lawyer has other people to pay and they can't do their best work for you if they're worrying about their next paycheck.

Educating Yourself about the Legal Process After Hiring Your Lawyer

170. After hiring your lawyer, meetings should be scheduled shortly thereafter. These meetings may include discussions about: the preparation and filing of your divorce petition or review of your spouse's divorce petition; the preparation of the response to your spouse's divorce petition; obtaining factual information from the client about the grounds for divorce, assets, debts, income, expenses, Interrogatories and Request for Production of Documents, depositions (possibly), mediation; preparation of the Marital Dissolution Agreement; Temporary and/or Permanent Parenting Plans; the Final Decree for Divorce; pretrial court appearances and a final court appearance.[5]

171. You need to gather the following documents and make copies for your lawyer: Prenuptial and Postnuptial Agreements; federal and state personal, corporate, and partnership tax returns; financial statements; mortgage documents; employment records; partnership and corporate agreements; cancelled checks and credit card charge records; retirement plans; IRAs; titles to all vehicles and boats; deeds to property; real estate appraisals; all insurance policies (life, health, homeowners, disability); bank account statements; savings account statements; investment account statements; inheritance and trust documents; wills; debts; and proof of misconduct by your spouse, including letters, videos, computer hard drives, e-mails, text messages, and photographs.[6]

172. Prepare and maintain a detailed factual history of your marriage. Include the good, the bad, and the ugly. This history should also contain issues regarding you and your spouse including adultery, gambling, alcohol use and abuse, drug use and abuse, pornography, physical and emotional abuse, discipline, disabilities, neglect and involvement in the children's lives.

⁓

173. You should gather copies of information documenting your involvement with the children, including doctors' and dentists' records, school records, and daycare records. Your marital history should also contain dates of significant events in the care of your children including daily routines, trips to the doctor and dentist, school activities, sports activities, and extracurricular activities. Gather all photos and videos of you and the children which show you as a good parent.[7]

174. The legal document that starts divorce proceedings is called a Petition or Complaint for Absolute Divorce.[8]   It contains grounds for divorce and requests for legal relief, including, but not limited to, custody, visitation, spousal support, child support, property and debt division, attorney fees, and court costs.[9]

❧

175. The party who files first typically achieves a tactical advantage. Ask your lawyer about any benefit gained by "winning the race to the courthouse."[10]

176. In many states, when a divorce complaint is filed, standard restraining orders automatically go into effect preventing both spouses from:

a) Transferring, assigning, borrowing against, concealing or disposing of the parties' assets and income

b) Increasing the debts except for reasonable and necessary living expenses

c) Canceling, modifying, or terminating insurance policies

d) Harassing, threatening, assaulting, or abusing the spouse and/or children

e) Making disparaging comments about your spouse to any person, including the children

f) Taking the children outside of the state and/or more than 100 miles away from the marital home (unless domestic violence in involved)[11]

177. Some spouses have lived as a married couple in more than one state. They may live in different states when divorce proceedings begin. The divorce may be properly filed in more than one state depending on each state's residency requirements. Before you file a divorce Complaint, you should consult with a lawyer in every state where the case could be filed to see which state laws will benefit you and your children the most.[12]

~&

178. Ask your lawyer about the grounds for divorce in your state. Be prepared to prove grounds for divorce before you file. Typical grounds for divorce include adultery, alcohol and/or drug abuse, gambling, inappropriate marital conduct, and cruel and inhuman treatment.[13]

179. Some states allow divorce based on "fault" grounds. In a fault-based case, a spouse must prove in court that he or she is entitled to a divorce based on the other spouse's improper conduct.[14]

180. Other states are "no fault" and do not consider the fault or misconduct of either spouse. A "no fault" divorce involves the parties reaching an agreement on all issues in the case and both parties signing a document known as a Marital Dissolution Agreement, and if children are involved, a Permanent Parenting Plan.[15]

181. In most cases, both parties claim grounds for divorce.[16] Remember, just because your spouse has accused you of misconduct does not mean it is true. Tell your lawyer if you have done anything that may give your spouse grounds for divorce.

182. Ask your lawyer if you have any defense to any of your spouse's claims for divorce because defenses will vary depending on the state you live in.[17]

❧

183. The spouse who files first is called the Petitioner or the Plaintiff. The other spouse is known as the Respondent or the Defendant.[18]

❧

184. Consider informing your spouse that you have filed for divorce before having a local sheriff serve papers on him or her. Don't have the sheriff serve divorce papers on your spouse solely to embarrass and/or harass him or her. Your spouse's lawyer may accept the divorce papers on his or her behalf.[19]

185. If your spouse has already filed divorce papers, you must file a formal document known as an Answer, which is your response to the allegations of your spouse's divorce Complaint unless your spouse has filed on "no fault" grounds commonly referred to as "Irreconcilable Differences." The responding spouse must admit as true or deny as untrue the factual allegations in the Complaint. Your Answer must be filed within 30 days of the date when the divorce Complaint is served on the defendant. The Counter-Complaint must be formally served on your spouse within 30 days.[20]

❧

186. You may want to ask your lawyer to file a Counter-Complaint or Counter-Petition against your spouse. In a Counter-Complaint or Petition, you may ask the court to award you any relief you want. It may contain the same and/or different grounds for divorce as alleged by your spouse.

187. In most states, "no fault" divorces cannot be granted until a waiting period of at least 60 to 90 days has passed after the divorce is filed. In contested or fault-based cases, the waiting period for a trial date may last from 3 to 24 months.[21]

188. A legal separation is a process that resolves all issues of divorce but the parties remain married. Legal separations are recommended in cases where a spouse is critically ill and cannot get health insurance coverage if the parties divorce. Most spouses who file Complaints for Legal Separation eventually end up divorced.[22]

189. Most states provide for orders of reconciliation that enable the parties to suspend the case for a period of time in order for the parties to resume their marital relationship.[23]

190. An annulment has the legal effect of invalidating a marriage as if the parties had never married. An annulment is granted only in rare cases. Most parties seek annulment for religious reasons.[24]

191. A same-sex marriage is also known as a gay or lesbian marriage. At this time, the federal government does not recognize same-sex marriages. Therefore, some rights are not available to same-sex couples, such as: social security benefits, veterans' benefits, hospitalization and health insurance, Medicaid, estate taxes, retirement savings, family leave, and immigration.[25]

192. Approximately 30 states have passed constitutional amendments banning same-sex marriages.[26] Legal marriages are defined in those states as a legal union between a man and a woman.[27] Currently, only a few states recognize same-sex marriages as legal civil unions or recognize same-sex marriages performed in other states. A few other states allow for same-sex domestic partnerships.

~&~

193. A couple in a valid same-sex marriage may also go through a legal divorce to end the relationship. Same-sex couples should seek legal and tax advice before they marry and before they divorce to educate themselves about the significance and repercussions of these issues.[28]

194. Common-law marriage is a union between couples who become legally married without a license or ceremony.[29] In a valid common-law marriage, the couple must have lived together for a significant period of time, and they must intend to marry. They must also hold themselves out to the public as a married couple. Only a few states recognize common-law marriages that occur in that state. Several states that do not recognize a valid common-law marriage having occurred in their state will recognize a valid common-law marriage from another state.[30] Spouses in valid common-law marriages must go through a legal divorce to end their relationship.

195. Cohabiting couples are members of either sex who simply live together but do not qualify as a common-law marriage. These couples do not have to go through a legal divorce to end their relationship. Assets acquired by the parties are generally divided under state law partnership principles.[31] For example, courts will look at who paid for the asset, who paid for the upkeep of the asset, the contribution of each party to the appreciation or loss of the asset, and how long the parties have had the asset. Issues of child custody and visitation will be addressed under state custody and visitation statutes that also apply to married couples.

196. A Marital Dissolution Agreement is a contract between the parties that represents the final settlement in a "no fault" case that divorces the parties, divides the property and debts of the parties. A Marital Dissolution Agreement may contain the party's agreement on the following issues: property, debts, retirement, alimony, custody, child support, life insurance, taxes, visitation, health insurance, attorney fees, and court costs.[32]

197. Most states have adopted laws that require parties with children to file a Permanent Parenting Plan that defines each party's obligations to provide for the custody and support of the children. Parenting plans typically contain issues such as custody, visitation, child support, transportation arrangements, school expenses, decision-making authority, income tax exemptions, medical insurance, life insurance, future disagreements or modification of the Parenting Plan, legal rights of the parents, and parental relocation of the children.[33]

~❧~

198. The terms of the Marital Dissolution Agreement and the Parenting Plan must be approved by the parties and the court to obtain a "no-fault" divorce on the grounds of Irreconcilable Differences.[34]

CUSTODY

199. Every state has laws that list criteria for awarding custody. In most states the legal standard for deciding which parent will get primary custody of the children is what arrangement is in the best interest of the children.[35]

⟡

200. In the past, the non-custodial parent (usually the father) typically had parenting time every other weekend, a few weeks in the summer, and every other holiday. This arrangement has changed dramatically in recent years. Today, parents are spending more equal amounts of time with their children during holidays, vacations, and the school year. In many states there is no preference or presumption that joint legal custody, joint physical custody, or sole custody will apply.[36]

201. Don't get caught up with the titles of "sole custody" or "primary custody." The most important issues are the amount of each spouse's parenting time with the children and each spouse's right to make significant decisions about the children.

202. Mothers don't automatically win custody cases. Fathers are being awarded primary custody with increasing frequency.

203. In joint custody arrangements, the primary residential parent is the parent with whom the children will live a majority of the time.[37] The primary custodian may have ultimate decision-making authority in the areas of education, non-emergency medical care, religion, and extracurricular activities. One parent may have ultimate decision-making authority in some areas of the children's lives, and the other parent may be responsible for decisions in other areas. The recent trend is that both parents have joint decision-making authority in all areas of the children's lives.

❧

204. Many judges award primary custody to the parent they believe has played the greater role in raising the children and who they believe will promote a positive working relationship with the other parent.

205. There are no real winners in custody fights. In most cases, they have a devastating effect on the parties and their children. The emotional and legal cost of custody trials is substantial. Custody battles should be avoided if at all possible.

❧

206. When formulating a visitation schedule, both parents must consider everyone's schedule, school time, extracurricular activities, sports, church, vacation, and work schedules. If the parents can agree on a visitation agreement, the court will usually approve it.[38]

❧

207. If you request substantial parenting time with your children, you better exercise it. If the other parent regularly refuses to visit the children, ask your lawyer about changing the visitation order.

208. Most states have statutes that calculate how child support is determined. Some of the issues that determine the amount of child support are: the number of children, the income of both parents, the total number of days each parent spends with the children, the cost of hospitalization and health insurance for the children, and the cost of daycare expenses and extracurricular activities for the children.[39]

❧

209. In most states, child support is paid until the child turns 18 years old or graduates with his or her high school class, whichever is later. If you have a special needs child, the court may order child support to be paid past the child's 18th birthday or graduation from high school.[40]

210. In some states, if the child's needs or parent's ability to pay child support substantially and materially changes, then the payment may be raised or lowered.[41]

❧

211. In some states, the court cannot order a parent to pay college tuition and/or other education expenses for a child. However, a parent may agree by contract to pay for college education expenses.[42]

❧

212. Ask your lawyer about the federal regulations that determine which spouse may claim the child(ren) as dependent exemptions for his or her tax returns.

213. Many parties believe they can go to Bankruptcy Court to avoid paying child support, spousal support, or other court-ordered payments. Recent changes in the Federal Bankruptcy laws have made it more difficult for parties to discharge any court-ordered support payments.[43]

214. If your spouse pays child support and/or spousal support, make sure a court order exists requiring the payer to maintain life insurance to cover the entire amount of the support payments if he or she dies before the support is paid in full.

215. Most states have laws that address the relocation of the primary parent and the children to another state or 100 miles or more from your home. In most cases, the courts require the moving parent to have a legitimate reason or a reasonable purpose for the move. An actual job transfer or better job opportunity usually provides a proper reason for the move. A new boyfriend or girlfriend is not a good enough reason to relocate, nor is relocating simply to avoid the other parent.[44]

216. The issue of who will receive the family pets has become increasingly common. In most states, pets are treated like other personal property such as household furniture and furnishings. Courts typically focus on such issues as the value of the pet, who paid for the pet, whether the pet was a gift, who primarily cared for the pet, and the children's relationship with the pet. Some courts are even awarding primary and/or shared custody and visitation privileges with pets by applying a traditional custody-type analysis of what arrangement is in the best interest of the pet and the family members.[45]

217. Marital Dissolution Agreements and Parenting Plans typically become final 30 days after the judge signs the documents. In most states, if you want to change the court order, you must file with the court a Motion to Alter and Amend the order within 30 days after the judge signs the documents.[46]

❧

218. In most states, if you want to appeal a court order, you must file a Notice of Appeal within 30 days after the judge signs the Final Order.[47]

219. In most states, final court orders for alimony, child support, and visitation may be modified only by proving a material change in circumstances occurring since the last court order.[48]

ALIMONY

220. Alimony is a form of spousal support that is based on the relative financial needs and income of the parties. Most states have laws that list the factors that a court should consider when awarding alimony.[49]

221. Ask your lawyer to explain the various types of alimony and which one may be appropriate in your case. Categories may include:

a) Transitional Alimony: temporary payments to enable a financially disadvantaged spouse to adjust to the financial consequences of a divorce.[50]

b) Rehabilitative Alimony: short-term payments to enable a financially disadvantaged spouse an opportunity to become financially self-sufficient.[51]

c) Alimony in Futuro: long-term payments for a spouse who is unable to achieve financial self-sufficiency.[52]

d) Alimony in Solido: a definite amount of support that is payable in one lump sum or paid in payments for a definite period of time.[53]

222. Ask your lawyer how much alimony you may get and how long it will last. Find out about the tax consequences for each type of alimony.

❧

223. Ask your lawyer whether alimony can be modified either before or after the divorce. In most states final court orders for alimony may be modified only by proving a substantial and material change in circumstances occurring since the last court order.

❧

224. If you are receiving alimony and/or child support, you should have life insurance on the payer's life in a sufficient amount to cover the full amount of alimony and/or child support if the payer dies prematurely.

225. Living with someone after the divorce, even if you are not romantically involved, may cause your alimony to be stopped or reduced. If an alimony recipient remarries, then the spousal support stops in most cases.[54]

DIVIDING ASSETS & LIABILITIES

226. Most assets acquired by the parties during the marriage are considered joint or marital property. Most debts incurred during the marriage are considered joint obligations.[55]

❧

227. Assets gifted, inherited, or owned by the parties before the marriage are typically considered that spouse's separate property. Ask your lawyer to explain the factors a court will consider when determining whether an asset is separate property.[56]

228. Most states have statutes that define what assets are considered joint or marital property. Ask your lawyer to explain what factors the court will consider when determining whether an asset is marital property.[57]

229. Most states have statutes that control property and debt division. Ask your lawyer to explain to you all the factors that the court will consider when dividing assets and debts.[58]

230. Be very careful when making an agreement that your spouse must pay any jointly titled debts, especially if he or she is financially irresponsible. On a jointly titled debt, the creditor can sue either party for the unpaid debt. Your creditors could care less about what a court order says about who must pay a debt. A creditor will come after whoever they believe can pay the debt.[59]

231. If you're concerned that your spouse will withdraw or transfer funds from a joint account or make excessive charges on the joint credit card, ask your lawyer about obtaining a restraining order.

232. If your spouse has had problems with the IRS, insist that he or she take responsibility for all payments, penalties, and interest that the IRS may assess against both of you as a result of filing a joint income tax return.

233. Ask your lawyer if selling certain assets (real estate, stocks, bonds, etc.) may create state and/or federal tax consequences. Ask about the tax consequences on any asset you receive.

234. Ask your lawyer if you are eligible to draw Social Security benefits on your account or your spouse's account.[60]

◦❧

235. Beware of signing a joint federal and or state income tax return with a soon-to-be ex-spouse. Have a competent accountant calculate your tax liability if you file tax returns jointly. Insist that your spouse indemnify and hold you harmless for any payment to the IRS that is your spouse's responsibility.

◦❧

236. Always remember that if your spouse moves out of the marital home, the same income that paid for one household must now pay for two households.

237. In many cases, it is difficult to get a judge to order a parent to move out of the marital home.

❧

238. If you are seeking custody of the children, do not move out of the marital home just because your spouse wants you to. If you want to move out, talk to your lawyer first. It may be difficult to move back in if you change your mind.

❧

239. If you've been the primary caretaker of your children, take them with you if you move out.

❧

240. Attorney fees are considered a form of alimony (spousal support). In most states, a judge may award attorney fees based on the financial needs and income of both parties.[61]

241. Just because your spouse asks for you to pay his or her attorney fees does not mean the judge will award it to them.

❧

242. Ultimately, you're responsible for paying all of your attorney fees unless agreed to by the parties or ordered by the court.

❧

243. A judge may order one party to pay all or part of his or her spouse's attorney fees. This is discretionary with most courts.

❧

244. A non-employee spouse may be eligible for federally mandated COBRA health insurance after the divorce. COBRA coverage can be expensive, so be sure to discuss this and other health insurance options with your lawyer.[62]

245. Some women take back their maiden name after the divorce is final, but women with children might choose to keep their married name to be consistent with the children's last name. For women who do change their names, they will need to notify the IRS, financial and commercial institutions, insurance agencies, and health care providers as soon as possible. They will also need to obtain a new Social Security card, driver's license, and credit cards. If they have children, they should notify the school and/or childcare authorities.[63]

Protecting Yourself

246. Electronic technologies are not always your friend. Remember that nothing on your computer that you look at or transmit on the internet is ever really private. Embarrassing writings, photos, videos, audio messages, and records of your online transactions can be retrieved and used against you.

247. For instance, never view a website that would embarrass you or send an e-mail, text message, or other communication that would embarrass you or hurt your case if the judge read it in court.

248. Never allow anyone to photograph or videotape you in an embarrassing or inappropriate situation. If photos, DVDs, and/or videotapes exist, put them in a secure place and call your lawyer.

❧

249. If you find copies of photographs or videotapes of your spouse in an embarrassing or inappropriate situation, take them to your lawyer.

❧

250. If you suspect your spouse has viewed inappropriate websites on the family or other jointly owned computer, ask your lawyer about hiring a forensic computer expert to make a copy of the computer hard drive.

251. You may be tempted to be an electronic spy, but don't do it. Your efforts can have serious legal consequences.

❧

252. Never install a recording or tracking device on your spouse's cell phone.

❧

253. Never install a recording and/or tracking device on your spouse's vehicle.

❧

254. Never install spyware software on your spouse's home or office computer.

❧

255. Never install a recording device on the home phones unless you obtain your spouse's permission in writing.

256. The Attorney/Client privilege requires lawyers to preserve as confidential all information, both written and oral, communicated by or on behalf of a client except under limited circumstances. Disclosure by the client of information protected by this privilege to anyone else may destroy the confidentiality of the information.

❧

257. Silence is golden when it comes to divorce. Watch what you say and be extremely careful about confiding important details of your case to anyone. Even your closest family members and friends can slip up and accidentally reveal something that could hurt your case.

❧

258. Never mention anything about your spouse and/or the divorce on the internet or any social network such as Facebook, MySpace, or Twitter.

259. Never record a conversation between you and your spouse without talking to your lawyer first. It is illegal in some states to record a conversation with your spouse unless you obtain their consent. Many states will allow a party to a conversation to record the conversation without the other party's consent. Ask your lawyer first.

260. Recorded messages left on answering machines, cell phones, voicemail, and other recording devices can be kept and used as evidence, especially if the call is abusive or threatening.

261. Never record a conversation with your children about the divorce without talking to your lawyer first.

262. Never record a conversation between your spouse and their boyfriend or girlfriend. It is illegal.

❧

263. Ask your lawyer before you install a "nanny cam" or any other video and/or audio recording device in your spouse's residence or vehicle.

❧

264. Until you are actually divorced, do not do anything that may give your spouse grounds for a divorce.

❧

265. Dating and intimate involvement while separated is considered adultery in many states. Do not date. If you do, chances are your spouse will find out.

266. Don't be seen in public alone with any person whom your spouse may suspect you are dating.

❧

267. If you are dating, never allow your picture to be taken or videotaped with your date. You may have to give the details under oath about your intimate involvement, trips you have taken together, and money you have spent on your boyfriend or girlfriend.

❧

268. If you believe your spouse is having an affair, you may want to hire a private investigator. Consult with your lawyer first.

269. If you suspect that your spouse has been unfaithful during the marriage, you should have a full medical examination to see if you have contracted any sexually transmitted diseases (STDs).

270. Never call your spouse's lawyer even if an emergency exists. Your spouse's lawyer is not working for you.

271. Should your spouse's attorney call you, tell him or her to contact your lawyer. It is unethical for your spouse's attorney to talk to you if you are represented by a lawyer.

272. Ask your lawyer before you close joint bank accounts and/or joint credit card accounts. Also ask your lawyer before you withdraw funds from a joint checking account, savings account, and/or brokerage account. This may be illegal.

❧

273. Ask your lawyer before you change the locks on your home, especially if your spouse still lives there.

❧

274. Ask your lawyer before you amend your Federal Income Tax form to increase your withholding from your earnings and reduce your net pay.

❧

275. Ask your lawyer before you make any withdrawals from an IRA, retirement plan, and/or pension plan.

276. You may legally get a copy of your own credit report, but never try to get a copy of your spouse's credit report. This is illegal.

❧

277. Ask your lawyer before changing your Last Will and Testament, Trust, Power of Attorney, Living Will, and/or any beneficiary of a will and/or trust. If you do not have a valid Last Will and Testament, Power of Attorney, and/or Living Will, ask your lawyer about preparing one.

❧

278. If it is your responsibility, never miss a mortgage payment or allow your spouse's and/or children's hospitalization and health insurance or life insurance to lapse.

279. Never hide assets. Somehow they just eventually show up.

~

280. Never threaten to file criminal charges against your spouse solely to gain an advantage.

~

281. Be cautious about signing any document or making any agreement suggested by your spouse that changes any court order. Consult with your lawyer because most verbal agreements between parties to modify a court order are unenforceable. Any change in a court order requires a new court order signed by the lawyers and the judge.[64]

282. Pay your child support and alimony on time. Never deduct the cost for a child's extracurricular, athletic, or school expense from your court ordered child support or alimony payments. Late payments or reduced alimony or child support payments may land you in jail.

❧

283. Consider paying alimony and child support by monthly automatic bank draft. If the alimony or child support payment is not made on time, it is not the payer's fault unless there is not enough money in the payer's account.

284. When you pay or receive child support and/or alimony, always keep a copy of every payment. If you pay by check, always write the month and year on the "for" line of every check because you may have to produce copies of every payment if your spouse accuses you of not paying. Note whether the payment is for alimony, child support or both. If you pay alimony and child support in the same check, the total amount must include the correct amount of alimony plus the correct amount of child support. In most judges' eyes, an underpayment of alimony and/or child support violates a court order. Be very careful.

285. If your ex-spouse does not make the alimony or child support payments on time, you can usually take them back to court and charge them with contempt of the court order.

286. Spouses who intentionally violate a custody and visitation order may go to jail.

DOMESTIC VIOLENCE

287. Domestic violence occurs more often than most people realize, affecting an estimated 3 to 4 million American households every year.[65]

❧

288. Children who are exposed to domestic violence tend to suffer anxiety, depression, and other trauma-related symptoms. They are more likely to have higher levels of aggression, anger, hostility, fear, and poor social relationships. They may also experience difficulties in school, and many experience cognitive or language difficulties.

289. Abusers usually repeat the same pattern of violence, and the frequency and intensity of the abuse tends to escalate over time.

❧

290. Divorces and legal separations often increase domestic abuse. Statistically, about half of all violent assaults occur at or soon after separation.

❧

291. Never tolerate emotional or physical abuse. Immediately remove yourself and your children from a dangerous situation. Don't be afraid to ask for help by calling the police. You could save your life and your children's lives by dialing 911.

292. If you are now or have been a victim of domestic abuse, talk to your lawyer immediately about obtaining a Restraining Order and/or an Order of Protection to protect you and your children.[66]

❧

293. Ask your lawyer about obtaining a court order to remove your abusive spouse from your household.

❧

294. Tell your lawyer if your spouse has falsely accused you of domestic violence in the past. A spouse who has made false claims before is likely to try it again.

❧

295. Your spouse may try to hit your "hot buttons" so that you will react in an abusive or violent way – don't do it.

296. Stay calm, especially in front of your children. Don't yell, scream, or throw things. Don't touch your spouse against his or her will in any way. Just blocking your spouse from entering or leaving a room may be considered abusive.

297. If the police answer a domestic violence call from your spouse, keep your cool and be as cooperative as possible. Police typically arrest the person they believe is the aggressor.[67]

298. If you are accused of committing an act of physical abuse, your spouse may obtain an Order of Protection against you that is based only on his or her story.

299. An Order of Protection is an extremely powerful tool. It's a court order that may remove a spouse from his or her house and may prohibit a spouse from having contact with the other spouse and his or her children. If you are under an Order of Protection, you must follow the court order.

❧

300. Willfully violating any court order, including an Order of Protection, can land you in serious trouble. A judge can send you to jail for disobeying an order; even just a phone call to your spouse is prohibited. People convicted of domestic abuse are usually sent to jail, where they belong.[68]

"HOLD ON TO YOUR HAT"

DISCOVERY
&
DEPOSITIONS

Interrogatories & Request for Production of Documents

301. Interrogatories and Request for Production of Documents are a series of written questions and requests for financial documents sent or received by your lawyer seeking information about the facts of your case.[69]

❧

302. Each party typically has 30 days to answer the other spouse's Interrogatories and Request for Production of Documents. Your lawyer and/or his legal assistant will likely help you prepare your answers.[70]

303. Interrogatories are always answered under oath. Your answers must be truthful. There is no excuse for a failure to tell the truth.

304. Carefully review, analyze, and critique every word of your answers. You cannot proofread your answers too many times. Proofread, proofread, and proofread again!

305. Every word of your answers may be used against you if they are inaccurate or untrue. Remember that every word of your answers – even innocent mistakes – can be used to prove that you are lying.

306. If you and your lawyer fully cooperate with your spouse's lawyer and provide full and complete disclosure, you will speed up the resolution of the case. If you and/or your lawyer intentionally delay responding to your spouse's discovery requests, you will quickly create distrust, which will make your case more difficult to resolve.

REQUEST FOR ADMISSIONS

307. Request for Admissions are a series of written questions that ask a spouse to admit the truth of certain facts. This typically follows the receipt of the answers to your spouse's Interrogatories and Request for Production of Documents.[71]

308. A spouse must respond in writing to all Request for Admissions within 30 days of receipt. If you fail to respond to the Request for Admissions within 30 days, then the court may rule that the factual allegations are true even if they are not.[72]

309. If you deny that a fact is true and your spouse's lawyer later proves that fact to be true, you may have to pay your spouse's attorney fees for the time required to prove the fact.[73]

DEPOSITIONS

310. A deposition is a formal proceeding, transcribed by a court reporter, which usually takes place in a lawyer's office where spouses and/or witnesses give testimony under oath.[74]

311. Your lawyer's primary goal is to pin your spouse down to a particular story so that if the story later changes, it will appear that he or she is dishonest. Your lawyer will also try to prove that your spouse's testimony is not only inaccurate but also untrue.[75]

⁓

312. Your lawyer should be present with you, and your spouse's lawyer should be present with him or her.

⁓

313. The spouses and any witnesses who are testifying can be asked questions by all lawyers present about any fact and/or issue that is legally relevant to the case. All witnesses should have their lawyers present during their testimony.

314. It is imperative that you make a good impression as a witness, because how you tell your story may be more important than what you say.

❧

315. Your goal is to convince your spouse's lawyer that you will be sympathetic, likeable, and a credible witness in court. You may get a better settlement offer if your spouse's lawyer believes you will make a good impression on the judge.

❧

316. The goal in deposition preparation is that you and your lawyer will not be surprised by any questions asked.

❧

317. You and your lawyer should discuss your strategies and the objectives of the deposition.

318. Plan to spend several hours with your lawyer to prepare for a deposition. Thorough preparation will boost your self-confidence.

319. Review carefully all Complaints, Answers, notes, Orders, Interrogatories, Request for Production of Documents, Request for Admissions and expert witness statements many times.

320. Pay particular attention to all documents personally signed under oath by you and your spouse.

321. Ask your lawyer about what questions he or she expects your spouse's lawyer to ask. Since no one can anticipate everything, be ready to answer all questions truthfully.

322. Ask your lawyer where to go, when to go, how to get there, what to bring, what not to bring, what to wear, and who will attend the deposition.

~&~

323. If you have any nervous habits that may be distracting, such as nail biting, fidgeting, and laughing inappropriately, tell your lawyer before the deposition.

~&~

324. Every word you say during a deposition may be used against you at trial.

~&~

325. Your story may be difficult, embarrassing, and humiliating, but you must always tell the truth under oath. If the judge thinks you are lying or hiding information, you will likely lose your case and damage your reputation.

326. In today's society, many people believe that lying under oath is okay. Lying is never okay, especially in the eyes of the judge.

327. It is easier to remember the truth. You will not always remember a lie.

328. If you realize you made a mistake or that one of your answers is inaccurate, correct your answer immediately.

329. You don't have to tell the whole story in a deposition, so don't volunteer information you haven't been asked for – even if you think it will help your case.

330. Resist the temptation to educate your spouse and his or her lawyer about how strong you think your case is.

❧

331. Don't be tempted to educate your spouse's lawyer about what you think they should know. Instead, make the lawyer ask for the information he or she wants.

❧

332. The more you say, the more you have to remember to defend as truthful and accurate.

❧

333. Listen carefully to each question, and don't try to answer until you fully understand the question.

334. Do not try to answer a question that you don't completely understand. Ask your spouse's lawyer to repeat the question.

$\sim$

335. Think about the question before you begin to answer. Never just "blurt out" an answer. Carefully scrutinize every word of your answer before it comes out of your mouth.

$\sim$

336. Answer just the question asked; don't ramble. Keep your answers short and to the point.

$\sim$

337. Don't volunteer an opinion unless it is specifically asked for, and don't make any statements that you are unsure of.

338. Never guess. Never speculate. Guessing is rarely accurate or truthful and can make you look deceptive.

❧

339. Never exaggerate or overplay your hand.

❧

340. If you are asked about a document, read it carefully even if you've already read it. Don't answer a question about a document unless you understand precisely what it says.

❧

341. Never volunteer to gather information or documents.

❧

342. It's okay to say you do not know the answer to a question.

343. Never answer a question in a smart aleck tone such as "you tell me!"

⤜

344. Resist answering a question with "I don't recall." "I don't know" or "I don't remember" sounds more believable.

⤜

345. Whenever you give an effective answer, your spouse's lawyer may try to make you change it. Stick to your guns. Don't apologize or try to justify what you said.

⤜

346. Listen very carefully before you agree that a statement made by your spouse's lawyer is true or untrue.

347. If you have finished your answer, resist the temptation to continue talking if your spouse's lawyer remains silent.

348. Beware of answering questions that include absolutes such as "always" and "never." For example, "Isn't it true that you always have more than one glass of wine at night?"

349. Don't let your spouse's lawyer put words in your mouth or try to testify for you.

350. You may be smarter than your spouse's lawyer, but don't try to outsmart or outfox him or her. That's the lawyer's game.

351. Never assume anything.

❧

352. Don't get distracted by trying to figure out why your spouse's lawyer asked a specific question or what the next question will be.

❧

353. Never let your guard down. Your spouse's lawyer will be watching every word you say and every move you make to discover the strengths and weaknesses of your case.

❧

354. Keep your cool. Don't let your spouse's lawyer anger you. Don't argue, and don't threaten. Your lawyer will protect you from aggressive questioning.

355. Your spouse's lawyer isn't your friend, even when he or she is extra nice. Avoid all small talk with everyone on your spouse's legal team.

❧

356. Never object to a question; that is your lawyer's job. Whenever a lawyer objects, stop talking. Your lawyer will tell you whether to continue.

❧

357. Speak in a strong, clear voice – not too fast. Don't answer by nodding or shaking your head or saying "uh huh." And don't use slang.

❧

358. Once a question has been asked by your spouse's lawyer, only you can answer it.

359. Never say anything or do anything during the deposition that would embarrass you if the judge read your testimony in court.

~&~

360. Be on your best behavior and don't answer in a sarcastic or derogatory manner. Never be rude or arrogant; curse or use inappropriate language; or yell or scream.

~&~

361. Should you begin to lose control of your emotions, tell your lawyer that you need to take a break.

~&~

362. Angry and volatile witnesses make mistakes.

~&~

363. If you get angry during the deposition, you will likely get angry at trial.

364. A written transcript will be prepared of your deposition testimony. Your lawyer should give you the opportunity to review your testimony to correct any mistakes.

❧

365. Always keep in mind how your deposition testimony will sound to your spouse, the lawyers, and the judge.

MEDIATION

366. Mediation is an out-of-court meeting where spouses and lawyers (if you have one) meet with a mediator to try and settle all issues of the divorce. The mediator is typically an experienced family law attorney who acts as a neutral third party.

367. Mediation has revolutionized domestic relations law. Today, divorce and child custody cases are settled in mediation with increasing frequency.

❧

368. In many states, mediation is ordered by the courts in all cases.[76]

❧

369. Mediation dramatically reduces the costs and time necessary to settle your case. The process is considerably less contentious than a trial. Settling a case in mediation can also help decrease the hostility between spouses. This is particularly beneficial if children are involved.

370. In mediation, spouses agree on a property settlement and/or parenting plan that meets their unique needs. Both parties control their settlement, unlike a court battle in which they lose all control over the final outcome.

371. Mediation is legally binding on the parties only if they agree to and sign a written settlement agreement and/or a Marital Dissolution Agreement and a Parenting Plan. Only the mediated agreement is filed with the court.

372. Ask your lawyer to explain the different types of mediation that are used in your area.

373. The most common form of mediation is called the "Caucus Method," where the parties stay in separate rooms with their lawyers, and the mediator goes back and forth negotiating with the lawyers and their clients. The mediator may also meet with the attorneys alone. The mediator is actively involved in reaching a settlement, makes recommendations based on the evaluation of each party's case, and advises the parties how the court is likely to rule.

❧

374. Your lawyer's primary goal is to convince the mediator that you will make a sympathetic, likeable, and credible witness in court and to provide the mediator with sufficient evidence that would persuade the judge to decide the case in your favor.

375. The goal in mediation preparation is that you and your lawyer will fully evaluate the strengths and weaknesses of your case and prepare the case as if you were getting ready for trial. You will need to discuss strategies and objectives in detail. You also need to try to anticipate your spouse's strategies and how to counter their arguments.

376. Plan to spend several hours with your lawyer to prepare for mediation. Thorough preparation will boost your self-confidence.

377. You will meet with your lawyer to prepare for the mediator a list of your assets and debts, a list of your monthly income and expenses, a proposed Marital Dissolution Agreement (settlement agreement), and a proposed Permanent Parenting Plan (if you have children), including a child support worksheet.

❧

378. You will also need to give your lawyer the most current financial records and all records regarding your children.

379. You and your lawyer should also discuss what documents to send to the mediator including copies of all Complaints and Answers, court orders, answers to all interrogatories, Request for Production of Documents and Request for Admissions, federal income and/or state tax returns, payroll records, appraisals of real property, business valuations, parenting assessments, evidence of fault of either party, transcripts of depositions of parties and witnesses, photographs, e-mails, tape recordings, and any other "smoking gun" evidence that may not be known to the other party.

❧

380. Before the mediation, your lawyer should prepare a mediation statement that sets forth the strengths and weaknesses of your case. Your statement should be drafted in a way to present your case in a light most favorable to you.

381. In most cases, mediation is no place for children. However, you and your lawyer should discuss whether it is advisable to include the children, their counselors and/or reports from their counselors, your counselors and/or their reports.

❧

382. You and your lawyer should also discuss what, if any, evidence provided to the mediator should not be shared with your spouse and his or her attorney. You don't want to educate the other side about the strengths or weaknesses of your case if the mediation is unsuccessful.

❧

383. Ask your lawyer where to go, when to go, how to get there, what to bring, what not to bring, what to wear, who will attend the mediation, and how negotiations will be conducted.

384. If you have any nervous habits that may be distracting to the mediator, such as nail biting, fidgeting, or laughing inappropriately, tell your lawyer before the mediation.

385. All evidence including communications, records, documents, and reports produced during mediation are confidential and privileged.[77] This means that the parties, the attorneys, and the mediator cannot disclose the evidence used in mediation except under narrow circumstances. This encourages the parties to fully disclose any sensitive information to the mediator to help settle the case.

386. During mediation, each party negotiates strongest for those issues that are the most important to him or her and compromises on the less important issues.

❧

387. Cases settled in mediation are less likely to be taken back to court after the divorce, and the parties are more likely to be satisfied with the results.

❧

388. The selection of a mediator is as important as your selection of a lawyer. Both attorneys must agree on the selection. Should they disagree, the court will choose.

389. Look for a mediator with a success rate of settling 90% or more of his or her cases. If possible, your mediator should have considerable family law court room experience and will have worked with the judge in your case.

390. Remember that a mediator's job is to settle your case. You must understand that the mediator is not going to be your advocate.

391. Approach mediation with an open mind and a willingness to compromise. Good faith on the part of everyone is essential to a successful mediation.

392. Every case has the potential for settlement, so don't assume your spouse won't settle.

393. When children are involved, parents must always honor their children by placing their best interest first. Love your children more than you dislike your spouse, and put what's important for them ahead of any personal animosity.

394. Tricks like asking for more parenting time in order to reduce child support are not the mark of a loving parent. Be true to your children's needs; their future is in your hands.

395. It is not advisable to attend mediation without being represented by a lawyer. Attending mediation alone could be disastrous for you and your family.

396. Don't bring a friend or family member to mediation unless your lawyer and the mediator agree. Even well-meaning friends and family can complicate your case.

❧

397. Leave your boyfriend or girlfriend at home. Just the presence of a new "significant other" at mediation can destroy any chance of success.

❧

398. It's normal to be tense during mediation, but a sense of humor can relieve the stress. It's okay to laugh at appropriate times – though never at the expense of someone else, including your spouse.

399. Be cordial to your spouse and his or her lawyer. Cordiality and common courtesy demonstrate strength and may increase the chance of a successful settlement.

❧

400. Cordiality by your lawyer should never be confused with disloyalty and is a successful negotiation tool.

❧

401. Character attacks on a spouse or his or her lawyer rarely produce positive results and can backfire on the attacker.

❧

402. Maintain your composure at all times.

❧

403. Always leave room for negotiation in every settlement proposal.

404. Making the first settlement proposal is a sign of strength, not weakness, and establishes the initial range of settlement favorable to you.

❧

405. Use your initial proposal to educate the mediator and your spouse about the strengths of your case.

❧

406. Some spouses will ask for the "stars" hoping for the "moon."

❧

407. Greed can get the best of some people, and their initial settlement proposals can be unreasonably high or low. Don't overreact.

408. Avoid fights over insignificant issues. Do you really want something, or are you just trying to keep your spouse from getting it?

❧

409. Remember to pick your battles wisely. Ask yourself if those monogrammed spoons or that old chainsaw is really worth going to court for. Be honest with yourself before you damage the mediation.

❧

410. You will need to decide what your "drop dead" point is. This occurs when you decide you would rather go to court than take your spouse's last offer.

411. Your "drop dead" point is usually a moving target. You may need to revise your "drop dead" points as the negotiation progresses.

❦

412. Arbitrary settlement deadlines are rarely effective.

❦

413. Never tell or indicate to your spouse that you do not want to go to court even if you don't. This will weaken your ability to negotiate. In order to get your spouse's best offer, he or she must believe that you are willing to end mediation and take your case to court.

❦

414. You must be willing to walk away from mediation to get what you want.

415. No matter what is happening, keep your "poker face" on during settlement negotiations. Whatever you are thinking, don't let the mediator or the other side see your reactions and feelings on your face.

◦❧

416. Don't expect to leave mediation with everything you wanted or in a good mood. Keep in mind that a successful mediation is almost always a lot less costly – in time, money, and heartache – than a battle in open court.

◦❧

417. If you are fortunate enough to settle some or all of your issues, the lawyers must draft a written settlement agreement that will be signed by all the parties and attorneys. The lawyers and parties should also sign a Marital Dissolution Agreement and/or Parenting Plan if the entire case settles.

418. Most courts will enforce a signed written settlement agreement, Marital Dissolution Agreement, and/or Parenting Plan even if a party tries to back out of the deal after the agreements are signed.

COURT HEARINGS

419. During the divorce, the parties and their attorneys address many issues. If agreements cannot be reached, then either attorney may request a pre-trial court hearing, and the judge will decide those issues. A judge may rule for you, for your spouse, or another way.

420. Family law judges are good people who try to do the right thing under very difficult circumstances.

421. Before you go to court, you and your lawyer need to know what you want to accomplish and how you want to do it.

❧

422. Overcrowded dockets give each party only a small amount of time to present their case during pre-trial hearings.

❧

423. Pre-trial hearings can be dangerous. An adverse ruling by a judge may make it more difficult to settle your case.

❧

424. Consider observing a pre-trial hearing in your judge's courtroom to help you understand how the legal process works.

425. You may bring friends and family to court hearings. Just like children, they need to be seen and not heard.

❧

426. Never bring your boyfriend or girlfriend to court.

❧

427. Never bring small children into the courtroom. If children cry or become cranky and unruly, their behavior may irritate the judge.

❧

428. Never let your cell phone ring in court. An annoyed judge may confiscate it.

❧

429. Text messaging or e-mailing in court often leaves an unfavorable impression.

430. Perception is not always reality, but judges are human. They don't know you and will be influenced by their perceptions in court. You want your judge to like you better than your spouse, so be on your best behavior at all times.

❧

431. Never do anything to create in the judge's mind an unfavorable impression.

❧

432. Never be rude or impolite in any way to a judge's court clerks, court officers, and court reporters.

❧

433. Good courtroom behavior begins in the parking lot. You never know who might be watching and listening.

434. Never show disrespect to your spouse or his or her lawyer. Treating them with kindness will work to your advantage.

❧

435. Never make a derogatory statement to anyone about your spouse, the judge, or your spouse's lawyer – someone will hear it.

❧

436. Always remember that judges, court officers, court reporters, and court clerks all talk to each other.

❧

437. Assume your judge knows nothing about your case.

❧

438. Your lawyer will tell the judge which facts are helpful to your case.

439. Don't think your case is special. The judge has likely heard cases involving worse misconduct than your case. For example, judges are not often shocked by adultery.

❧

440. Don't expect the judge to feel sorry for you. If the judge feels sorry for your lawyer, get a new one. If your lawyer loses credibility with your judge, hire another one.

❧

441. Never send the judge a letter, e-mail, or text message regarding your case.

❧

442. Get to court 30 minutes early. If you are delayed at all, call your lawyer immediately.

443. Don't worry if the judge is late. It is his or her court.

◦❧

444. Judges may forget much and forgive more, but they never forget or forgive a client's dishonesty. Just as there is no such thing as being a little bit pregnant, there is no such thing as being a little dishonest. Honesty is truly the best policy. Make that your guiding star.

◦❧

445. Be honest, and tell the truth. If you lose credibility with the judge, you will have to fight an uphill battle to regain his or her trust.

◦❧

446. Judges will be very angry if you lie, especially about your new boyfriend or girlfriend.

447. Judges can spot insecurity quicker than anyone. A judge who believes you are lying about anything is very likely to rule against you and may find you guilty of perjury.

❧

448. Stand up straight, and look the court officer in the eye when taking the oath.

❧

449. Always sit up straight while testifying.

❧

450. Speak clearly, and don't slur your words.

❧

451. Make eye contact with the judge.

452. Your conduct in court may be as important as your testimony. Always be on your best behavior.

453. Judges are not impressed with people who act frustrated, get angry, rant and rave, or try to stare them down (especially after a negative ruling).

454. If your judge asks you a question, answer what they ask, not what you want to tell.

455. Never interrupt the judge.

456. Never assume a judge has made a decision until his or her final ruling is made.

457. Don't refuse to answer a question unless your lawyer tells you to. Never answer a question with a question.

458. Stay calm and collected at all times. Emotional outbursts can destroy your case.

459. Compose yourself and take a deep breath before you begin answering any question or making any statement.

460. Drama queens (or kings) make themselves appear foolish in court. Don't look or act bored or arrogant. Such behavior may sink your case.

461. It is okay to cry, just not that much. Judges see tears every day. Crying must be legitimate.

462. Never raise your voice.

463. Never signal to a witness how to answer a question.

464. Never allow one of your witnesses, friends, or family members to "make faces" or "stare" at your spouse in court.

465. Don't cross your arms, wave your arms, shake your fists, or point at anyone.

466. Don't grab or pull your lawyer's arm to get his or her attention. Just pass them a brief note.

❧

467. If you don't get a good result in court, keep yourself under control. An emotional outburst in the courthouse is never to your advantage.

HOW TO DRESS IN DEPOSITIONS, MEDIATIONS, & IN COURT

468. Whenever you make an appearance during your case, how you look matters. The way you look will affect how others – the judge, mediator, your spouse's legal team, and witnesses – think about you and your case.

469. Always dress appropriately. No matter how casual or colorful your normal style is, you should choose clothing and accessories that show respect and seriousness of purpose for every legal proceeding you attend.

470. Don't wait until the last minute. Select your clothing and accessories the day before any deposition, mediation session, or court appearance.

471. From head to toe, good grooming always makes a good impression. Be neat, clean, and conservative in every aspect of your appearance.

472. Keep your hairstyle simple and conservative. A recent wash, cut, and styling makes for a neat look. So does a dye job to restore the natural look of hair that has been colored pink, green, or any other bright shade.

❧

473. Don't wear sunglasses or hats. Anything that hides or distracts from your face can create a negative impression. You can wear regular glasses if you need them, but sunglasses make you seem secretive. Hats, including baseball caps, can cast dark shadows and make you appear as if you are trying to hide something.

❧

474. If you have body piercings, remove body jewelry or cover piercings. Conceal tattoos with clothing or makeup.

475. Keep your hands away from your mouth. No food or drinks. Never chew gum, tobacco, or toothpicks. Don't suck on mints or hard candies. Try hard not to bite or chew your nails.

476. If you must smoke during a break, walk away from the courthouse and don't let any court personnel see you.

477. Wear your wedding ring if you have worn it throughout the marriage.

WOMEN

478. Choose a conservative dress, skirt, or trouser outfit that isn't too short or too tight. Never wear miniskirts, shorts, or cut-off shorts.

479. Never wear tight t-shirts or skimpy or strapless tank tops.

☙

480. Always wear appropriate undergarments – a bra, underwear, and a slip if necessary.

☙

481. Wear suitable, comfortable shoes, either flats or heels. Heels should be no higher than 3 inches.

☙

482. Don't wear tennis shoes, flip flops, sandals, or slides.

☙

483. Never overdo your accessories. At most, choose a simple necklace, a watch, and one pair of earrings. Stick with plain gold or pearl earrings – no dangles, drops, or large hoops.

484. Keep your makeup to a minimum when you're in a legal setting of any kind; less is always more.

❧

485. Wear light-colored lipstick and pale or clear nail polish. Bright red lipstick can give the wrong impression, and bright and fancy nails are distracting.

❧

486. If it is in your budget, you may want to consider hiring someone to do your hair and makeup the morning of your deposition, mediation, or court. Be clear that you want a conservative look.

❧

487. A strong scent can be overpowering, so avoid heavy perfume, cologne, and other scented body products.

MEN

488. If you plan to wear a suit, choose a well-fitting, conservative style in black, dark blue, or gray.

489. Dark dress pants – gray, black, or blue – worn with a conservative sport coat in a matching color will do as well as a suit.

490. If you don't have an appropriate suit or pants and jacket, try borrowing from a friend.

491. Never wear blue jeans, baggy or low-riding pants, shorts, or cut-offs.

492. Always wear a belt.

❧

493. Wear a white, long-sleeved dress shirt, and keep it tucked in. No t-shirts, tank tops, or muscle shirts.

❧

494. Choose a conservative tie. Avoid bright colors and bold patterns.

❧

495. Wear black or brown, hard sole, lace-up shoes (freshly shined) with dark socks. No tennis shoes, flip flops, sandals, or slides, and no white socks.

❧

496. Shave well and be sure any facial hair – mustache, beard, or goatee – is neatly trimmed.

497. Don't wear necklaces, earrings, or
bracelets. Wearing a wedding ring
and/or a watch is okay, but leave
other jewelry at home.

❧

498. Never wear strong aftershave,
cologne, body splashes, or other body
products with heavy scents.

FINAL THOUGHTS

499. Protect your good name; it's your most valuable asset.

⌣

500. If a person wants to protect his/her reputation, he or she must be concerned to some degree about what others think.

⌣

501. Take charge of your attitude. Be positive and don't waste your time blaming yourself or others.

⌣

502. Bad times don't last forever. Good times don't last forever.

⌣

503. Make peace with the past. Learn from your mistakes and turn them into opportunities for positive change.

504. Learn to forgive yourself and your spouse.

505. Pain and disappointment are part of life, but smiling and laughing can help you through those tough times.

506. Be a little kinder than necessary. Kindness to others will lift your spirits.

507. Never be afraid to apologize. Apologizing is a sign of strength, not weakness.

508. Learn to disagree without being disagreeable.

509. Take control of your life and set appropriate boundaries with your ex-spouse.

❧

510. Family and friends don't last forever. Never miss an opportunity to tell them how much they mean to you.

❧

511. Value your friendships. Rekindle friendships you have lost.

❧

512. Time can heal. Scars will remain. Never be ashamed of them.

❧

513. Never underestimate the power of words and actions to heal relationships.

514. Never give up on those who have disappointed you. Life is full of surprises.

515. It is best to create in your children's mind a positive image of yourself and your ex-spouse.

516. Live so that when your family and friends think of fairness, honesty, and integrity, they think of you.

517. Remember that life's most treasured moments are always centered around relationships, not things.

END NOTES

[1] Anita Cutrer, *Tips for Settling Your Divorce Case Through Mediation*, http://www.divorcemag.com/articles/Mediation/tips_settling_mediation.html (last visited Dec. 9, 2010).

[2] LARRY RICE, *The Complete Guide to Divorce Practice, Forms and Procedures for the Lawyer*, 59 (ABA Publishing 3d ed. 2005).

[3] James G. Carr, *A Judge's Guide to Protecting Your Reputation*, 36 LITIGATION 26, 26 (Spring 2010).

[4] *Id*. at 30.

[5] Rice, *supra* note 2, at 72.

[6] *Id*. at 77-78.

[7] *Id*. at 77.

[8] TENN. R. CIV. P. 3.

[9] TENN. CODE ANN. § 36-4-106 (2009).

[10] Rice, *supra note* 2, at 48-49.

[11] TENN. CODE ANN. § 36-4-106(d).

[12] *Id*. § 36-4-104.

[13] *Id*. § 36-4-101.

[14] *Id*. § 36-4-114.

[15] *Id*. § 36-4-103.

[16] *Id*. § 36-4-106.

[17] *Id*. § 36-4-120.

[18] Rice, *supra* note 2, at 49.

[19] *Id.*

[20] TENN. CODE ANN. § 36-4-110.

[21] TENN. CODE ANN. § 36-4-103: Rice, *supra* note 2, at 75.

[22] TENN. CODE ANN. § 36-4-102: Rice, *supra* note 2, at 48.

[23] TENN. CODE ANN. § 36-4-126: Rice, *supra* note 2, at 48.

[24] TENN. CODE ANN. § 36-3-101 – 113 ;case; Rice, *supra* note 2, at 48.

[25] Ralph Randazzo, *Elder Law and Estate Planning for Gay and Lesbian Individuals and Couples*, 6 Marq. Elder's Advisor 1 (2004).

[26] Tara Siegel Bernard, *Seven Tips for Dissolving Gay Unions,* N.Y. Times, Bucks Blog, Nov. 18, 2009, http://bucks.blogs.nytimes.com/2009/11/18/gay-divorce-part-2/.

[27] TENN. CODE ANN. § 36-3-113.

[28] Bernard, *supra* note 26: *Goodridge and You,* Divorcenet.com, http://www.divorcenet.com/states/massachusetts/goodridge_and_you.

[29] *Common Law Marriage* FAQ, NOLO, http://www.nolo.com/legal-encyclopedia/faqEditorial-29086.html (last visited Dec. 9, 2009).

[30] TENN. CODE ANN. § 36-3-306: *Troxel v. Jones*, 322 S.W.2d 251 (Tenn. Ct. App. 1958).

31. *Martin v. Coleman*, 19 S.W.3d 757, 761 (Tenn. 2000).

32. TENN. CODE ANN. § 36-4-103.

33. *Id.* § 36-6-404.

34. *Id.* § 36-4-103.

35. *Id.* § 36-6-106.

36. *Id.* § 36-6-101.

37. *Id.* § 36-6-402(4).

38. Rice, *supra* note 2, at 64.

39. *Id.* § 36-5-101.

40. *Id.* § 36-5-101(k).

41. *Id.* § 36-5-101(g).

42. *Pylant v. Spivey*, 174 S.W.3d 143, 151 (Tenn. Ct. App. 2003).

43. 11 U.S.C. § 523(a)(15) (2006).

44. TENN. CODE ANN. § 36-6-108.

45. Tabby T. McLain, *Pets in Divorce Overview*, Animal Legal & Historical Center, http://www.animallaw.info/articles/ovuspetcustodyindivorce.htm (2009).

46. TENN. R. CIV. P. 58, 59.

47. TENN. R. APP. P. 4.

48. TENN. CODE ANN. § 36-6-101(a)(2)(B).

49. *Id.* § 36-5-120.

50. *Id.* § 36-5-121(g)(2).

51. *Id.* § 36-5-121(e)(3).

52. *Id.* § 36-5-121(f)(1).

53. *Id.* §36-5-121(h).

54. *Rogers v. Rogers*, 795 S.W.2d 667, 668 (Tenn. 1990); Rice, *supra* note 2, at 58.

55. TENN. CODE ANN. § 36-4-121(b)(1)(A).

56. *Id*. § 36-4-121(b)(2).

57. *Id*. § 36-4-121(c).

58. *Id*. § 36-4-121(a).

59. *Long v. McAllister-Long*, 221 S.W.3d 1, 10 (Tenn. Ct. App. 2006).

60. Rice, *supra* note 2, at 82-83.

61. *Sullivan v. Sullivan*. 107 S.W.3d 507, 512 (Tenn. Ct. App. 2002).

62. Rice, *supra* note 2, at 59.

63. Rice, *supra* note 2, at 68.

64. Rice, *supra* note 2, at 82.

65. Id. at 50.

66. TENN. CODE ANN. § 36-3-601 et seq.

67. Id. § 36-3-601: Rice, *supra* note 2, at 50.

68. TENN. CODE ANN. § 36-3-610: Rice, *supra* note 2, at 50.

69. TENN. R. CIV. P. 33-34.

70. TENN. R. CIV. P. 33.01, 34.01.

71. TENN. R. CIV. P. 36.01.

72. TENN. R. CIV. P. 36.02.

73. TENN. R. CIV. P. 37.03.

74. TENN. R. CIV. P. 30.

75. Rice, *supra* note 2, at 92.

76. TENN. CODE ANN. § 36-4-131.

77. *Id*. § 36-4-130.

About the Author

John Hollins, Jr., has represented more than a thousand clients in divorce and domestic relations cases since 1987. Now president of the law firm of Hollins, Raybin & Weissman, P.C. in Nashville, Tennessee, John is also a family law mediator. He is a Fellow of the American Academy of Matrimonial Lawyers, has served on the Board of Professional Responsibility of the Supreme Court of Tennessee, is listed in "The Best Lawyers in America" and in "The Mid-South Super Lawyers," and holds the highest rating from Martindale-Hubbell. John and his wife live in Brentwood, Tennessee and are the parents of twin daughters.